I LIKE YOU

(a little book of friendship)

Sandy Gingras

**Andrews McMeel
Publishing, LLC**

Kansas City

08 09 10 11 12 TWP 10 9 8 7 6 5 4 3 2 1

ISBN-13: 978-0-7407-7375-4
ISBN-10: 0-7407-7375-5

Library of Congress Control Number: 2008921090

www.andrewsmcmeel.com

www.how-to-live.com

for
girlfriends

I like you because
of this and that...
because of what you
don't and do... but
mostly because of
who you are
through and through...

When there is a
chance of happiness
(or ice
cream)
in
the
air...

You say, "Yes! Let's
go for it." As if
"yes" were the most

natural of words.
I like you because
you are yes-y
and brave...

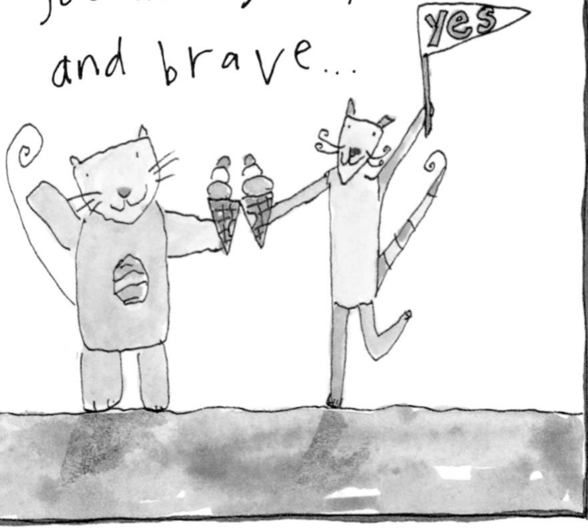

and because, left up to my own devices, I can be a big chicken about life.
no... nope... I can't just now...

you help me to balance life, and I help you to do the same...

When the hard rains
fall, I hold an
umbrella for you.

And when
the future
gets foggy,
you hold hopeful
signs for me.

We're friends, and I like you yesterday, today, and tomorrow too.

And other days,
we open up in the sun.
and then I felt...
I know how you feel...

Most days,
we just go on
and on...

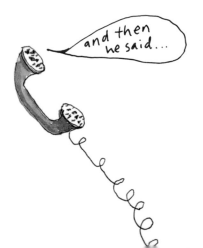

Sometimes, we dress up in dressy clothes

and dangerous shoes

And, although we don't say
anything bad at the time...

afterwards,
we
laugh very hard
about
our worst dates
and
bad mistakes.

I like being friends
with you when the
rain pitter-patters
the roof,

and when the
daffodils pop.

I like being friends with you when the snow is good for making snowballs,

sshhh... here he comes...

and we make piles to hide behind and throw at Tootles the dog when he walks by...

but sometimes
I just
like
to be
alone.

But then, you always get bored first and you come and knock on my door and say, "Come out, come out, wherever you are..."

and
I like that
too.

Sometimes, I feel grumpy & ugly

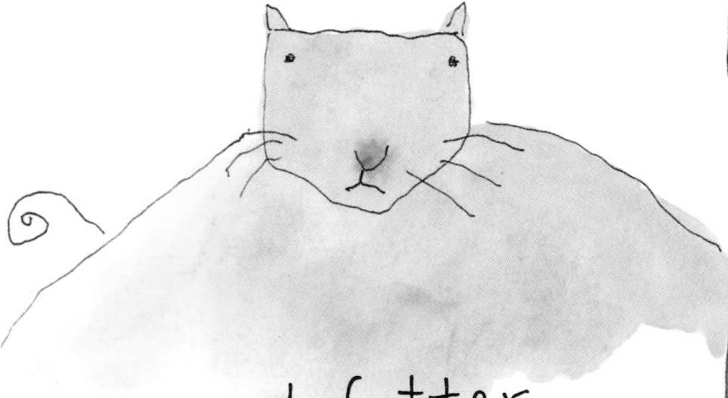

and fatter than I really am

because silliness

is a lifesaver.

you help me forget about
myself and remember

the BiGGer PicturE

Well, I like that more than you do, but you come along for the ride (even though I ask you to carry the bait)...

and even though
you don't like water
so much. "Yuck," you
say, "Yuck and yuck."
But you come anyway.

   And later, I go
on the Ferris wheel
with you...

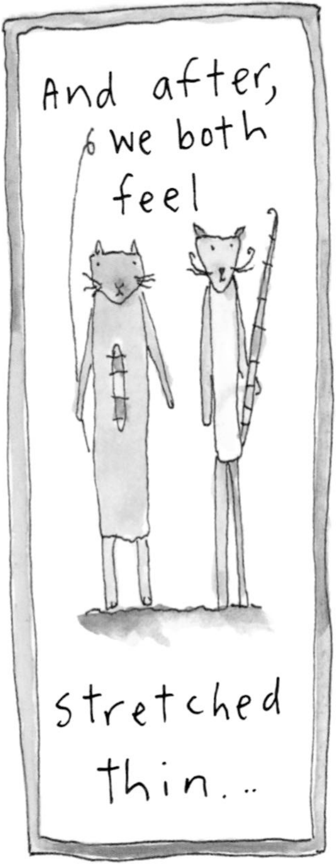
And after,
we both
feel
stretched
thin...

"Whew!" we say.

Being friends can be

tiring.

Sometimes, we don't see each other for a long, long time.

I'm on the island
of leave-me-alone

or you're in the city
of work-work-work

or one of us is
lost in the maze
of so-in-love.

But I know that
if I had a sad something
happen to me, you
would

zoom to my side...

and you would make a nice cup of tea and we would sip-sip all hokey-yokey like little old ladies
Suga

and you would say,
"Uh-huh... ummm, I know,
I know..." soft words
that would fall all
around me like rain

on a lake

because you
understand how
peaceful rain
on a lake sounds.

And, if you ever fell into a big hole, you know I wouldn't say, "that's that!" and walk away.

I would climb down to help you even if there was only a rope ladder (I don't like rope ladders) and I would help you up.

Everyone knows you can't leave a friend in a big hole.

And I know that
if I ever got lost

at sea

even though
the ocean is big

(especially for
someone afraid of
water).

And you would say, "You're not as lost as you think you are."

But being friends
with you isn't all
peaches and cream.

There are days
I truly dislike
your snippy ways.
And I find the
way you truffle
into your snuffles
downright awful...

Sometimes you think I'm not so sporty either.

Then, I think:
who needs friends
anyway?

I don't have the
time or energy for
that stuff...

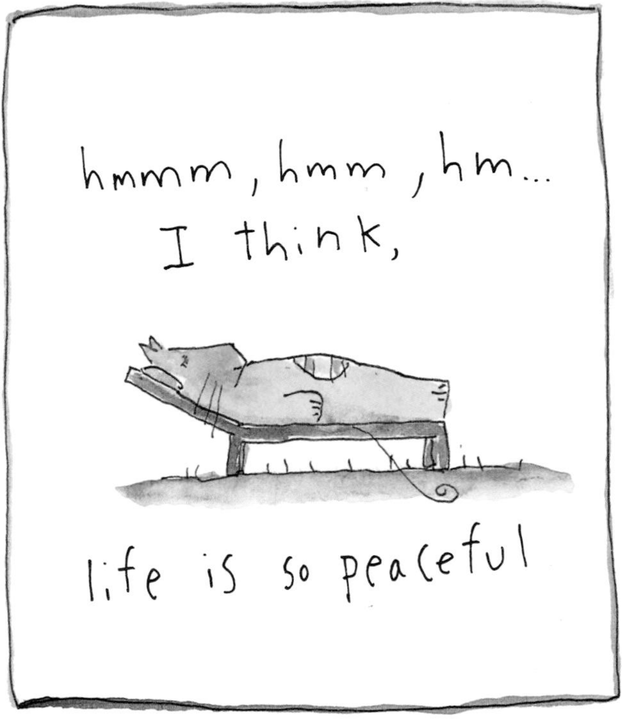
hmmm, hmm, hm...
I think,
life is so peaceful

but peaceful isn't
always all it's
cracked up to be.

A lot of things
seem

out of balance

and the world seems somehow harder

and after a while,
even the best
reason to be angry
begins to make
no sense at all.

Sometimes
we talk
and
talk
to make it
all ok again

or you bump into me
in the cereal aisle of
the super-mart and we
say hi-hi, I missed you
boo-hoo and our anger
just melts away
like it was nothing...

because

friendship

is
bigger than

anger

and we say, "Let's never fight again!" And we nod, but we don't really mean it, because we're just us (not some icky-perfect-goody-two-shoes people who smile all the time and never get mad).

we have
flaws
&
fizzles
&
foibles.

we're friends.

you like my big &
moody heart.

and we'll be friends until the end of always... because liking is a thing that grows and grows (even through the hard parts).